FROM VICTIM TO VISIONARY:

A Simple Guide to Starting Your Business After Trauma

BY BUKOLA ORIOLA

All rights reserved. No portion of the book thereof can be used or reproduced in any form except short quotes in the media for news purposes without written permission from the Publisher.

From Victim to Visionary: A Simple Guide to Starting Your Business After Trauma

Printed in United States

Copyright © 2025 by Bukola Oriola

ISBN: 978-1-955276-04-7

Published by:
Bukola Oriola Group, LLC
www.bukolaoriola.com/bukolaoriolagroup

Mailing address:
2168 7th Ave, Box 922
Anoka, MN 55303
Email: bukolaoriolagroup@bukolaoriola.com

Cover picture credit: canva.com

Dedication

I dedicate this book to God Almighty.

To every survivor who has ever felt unseen, unheard, or unworthy, this book is for you.

May you rise, rebuild, and reclaim your story with power. You are not just a survivor.

YOU are a visionary!

You Already Have What You Need. You might not believe it yet, but you already have:
- *Strength*
- *Wisdom*
- *Experience*
- *Passion*

Acknowledgments

To my fellow survivors, your courage is the foundation of this book.

To every mentor, friend, and supporter who walked beside me as I built this vision, thank you for believing in me.

To my community, thank you for showing up, for sharing your stories, and for inspiring me to continue this work every single day.

This book is possible because of you.

You get to build something that honors all of who you are.
From trauma to triumph.
From pain to purpose.
From victim to visionary.

Introduction

You Are Not Alone

I know what it's like to feel broken, silenced, and unsure of what the future holds. I also know what it means to rise again, not just to survive but to build, dream, and lead.

If you are reading this, you may have lived through something that tried to steal your voice, your hope, or your sense of purpose. But here is the truth: you are still here, and that means something. It means you have got something powerful inside you, something the world needs.

This book is for survivors like you. Survivors of human trafficking, domestic violence, abuse, or any life experience that left a scar. You are not a statistic. You are a visionary. You can create something beautiful from your pain - a business that reflects your truth, your healing, and your future.

And you don't need to have a business degree. You don't need a big budget or fancy website. All you need is the desire to start, the willingness to grow, and the belief that your story matters.

Let's take this step together. One page, one chapter, one breath at a time.

*Your business should heal you, not hurt you.
You don't have to push.
You don't have to hide.*

Chapter 1

You Are Not Just a Survivor. You Are a Visionary!

Let me tell you something important: You are not just what happened to you. You are creative. You are wise. You are strong. I call you a visionary, someone who can see beyond the pain and imagine something new. A better life. A new future. A business that helps others, supports your healing, and gives you freedom.

When I started my first business, I didn't have all the answers. I didn't know what I was doing. But I knew one thing: I wanted more. I wanted to use my voice, not just for me, but for others who felt voiceless. That's when things began to change.

And guess what? You don't have to wait until you "have it all together." You can start messy. You can start small. You can start right where you are.

What Is a Visionary Business?

A visionary business is not just about making money (though money is a good thing!). It is about creating something that matches who you are and where you are going. It could be:
- A hair care line that makes people feel confident.
- Whatever it is, it starts with your heart.
- A nonprofit that teaches others about healing.
- A speaking business that shares your lived experience expertise with the world.
- A cleaning service that helps others feel safe and cared for.

You Already Have What You Need. You might not believe it yet, but you already have:
- Strength
- Wisdom
- Experience
- Passion

And those are the real tools to start a business. Everything else like paperwork, marketing, and money can be learned. And I will walk you through it in the pages ahead.

Action Steps: Visionary Starter List

Now, take your first small step today. Are you ready? Just write down your thoughts. No pressure. Just you and your dream.

1. What do you care deeply about?

    (Helping people? Creating beauty? Making people feel safe?)

2. What are some things you have been through that made you stronger?

    (These can become your message or mission.)

3. What are some things people always ask you for help with?

    (This can point to your skills or potential business ideas.)

You don't need to have it all figured out. You just need to start.

You are not just a survivor. You are a visionary. And the world needs what you are about to build.

*You're not just building a business.
You're building hope.
And it starts with purpose.*

Chapter 2

Turn Your Pain into a Purpose-Driven Business

You have been through something hard, maybe even something that almost broke you. But you are still here. That means you have a purpose. And that purpose can become the foundation of a powerful business. A purpose-driven business is one that is born out of your heart. It is built from your story, your struggles, and your desire to help others. And that is what makes it different. That is what makes it special.

When I started speaking out about my experience as a survivor of human trafficking, I didn't do it to become "a businesswoman." I did it because I wanted to help someone else not go through what I went through. And from that pain, a purpose was born. Then came books, speaking engagements, workshops, and eventually my own company. I started my business as Bukola Braiding & Beauty Supply in 2007 while living at the battered women's shelter with my baby who was less than a year old. Your story can create something too.

Your Story Has Power

You may be thinking, "Why would anyone want to hear my story?" Let me tell you, someone needs your story. People connect with real people. When you share your truth, you give others permission to heal too. That connection builds trust, and trust builds business.

Maybe you:
- Overcame abuse and want to support other women
- Know how to navigate life after trauma and want to teach others
- Found healing in creating things such as hair products, candles, art, food, and want to share it

That is the purpose. That is power.

From Pain to Purpose, Step by Step
You don't need to have a grand plan. You just need to be open. Here is how you can start turning your pain into purpose:
- Think about the moments that changed you.
  What lessons did you learn? What helped you grow?
- Ask yourself who needs that wisdom.
  Is it young women? Single moms? Teen boys? Survivors?
- Think about how you can help.
  Can you teach? Create? Serve? Sell? Speak?

Your purpose is where your story meets someone else's need.

Real Example

Let's say you went through depression after leaving an abusive relationship. Now, you create self-care boxes with calming tea, candles, and affirmations. You are not just selling products, you are offering peace, because you've needed it too. Or maybe you grew up feeling like you had no voice. Now you run workshops teaching kids how to speak up and believe in themselves. Your pain does not disqualify you. It qualifies you.

Action Steps: Finding Your Purpose
Get a notebook or use your phone. Take a few minutes to reflect.
- What are 3 hard things you've been through?
  (Don't worry. No one has to see this but you.)
- What did you learn from each of them?
  (Think of one small lesson from each.)
- Who do you feel called to help?
  (This could be a specific group or just "people like me.")
- What is one way you could help today?
  (Encourage someone, share a tip, write a post, brainstorm a product.)

Starting a business from your story doesn't mean staying stuck in it. It means using it to grow, like a flower that blooms from the dirt.

You're not just building a business.

You're building hope.

And it starts with purpose.

Your business doesn't have to be big or perfect. It just has to be real and aligned with who you are. You get to choose:
- *Something you do with your hands*
- *Something you offer with your heart*
- *Something you create from your life*

That's what makes it yours.

Chapter 3

Find a Business Idea That Fits You

Now that you know your story has power and purpose, let's talk about what kind of business fits you. Because here's the truth: Your business should fit your life, not the other way around. You don't have to chase someone else's dream. You don't have to hustle 24/7. You can build something that works with your healing, your schedule, and your strengths. And yes, it can still make money.

What's Already In Your Hands?
Sometimes, we think we have to get more degrees or wait until we have "healed more" before we can start. But often, your business is already hiding in your everyday life. Take a look at what is already in your hands:
- What do people always ask you for help with?
  (Haircare tips? How to cook a certain dish? How you stay organized?)
- What do you love doing that feels natural?
  (Writing? Speaking? Making things with your hands?)
- What do people thank you for?
  (Encouragement? Cleaning help? Advice?)

Real Ideas from Real Survivors

Here are some real business ideas that survivors have started:
- A cleaning company that gives jobs to other women leaving abuse, men and youth who need jobs.
- A handmade jewelry shop with messages of hope
- A meal prep service for single moms
- A nonprofit that teaches kids about self-worth
- A haircare line made from homemade herbal recipes
- A speaker who educates communities about trafficking and healing

Your business doesn't have to be huge. It just has to be honest and helpful.

How to Brainstorm Your Fit
Let's do a little thinking together. Grab your notebook again or just say these out loud.

- What do I enjoy doing, even if I'm tired?
  (This could be a sign of a passion.)
- What have I learned the hard way that I could teach someone else?
  (Your story is your curriculum.) Mind you, your story does not mean sharing your tragic experiences.
- What problem do I know how to solve for someone?
  (This is how business begins, by solving a problem.)
- What type of work would make me feel proud?
  (This helps align your business with your values.)

What do I Know/or Do Well	What do I love Doing	What I Have Been Through	Business Idea
Making Skincare	Helping women feel confident	Hair loss after trauma	Natural haircare products
Writing	Sharing my story	Surviving trafficking	Speaking & book writing

What do I Know/or Do Well	What do I love Doing	What I Have Been Through	Business Idea
Cooking Healthy Meals	Encouraging others	Healing from abuse	Meal prep for survivors

Try filling in this chart for yourself.

Your business doesn't have to be big or perfect. It just has to be real and aligned with who you are. You get to choose:
- Something you do with your hands
- Something you offer with your heart
- Something you create from your life

That's what makes it yours.

Don't worry about getting it perfect. Just get it going. The most important thing is to choose a path that gives you:
- Freedom to grow
- Room to breathe
- A way to serve without burning out

Whether you are for-profit or nonprofit, you are still doing something powerful.

Chapter 4

Should You Start a For-Profit or Nonprofit?

Let's say you've got your business idea in mind. Maybe it's selling a product you love or helping others through your story. Now the big question comes up: Should I start a for-profit or a nonprofit? It is okay if this sounds confusing at first. We are going to break it down simply, so you can decide what fits your life, your mission, and your vision.

What Is a For-Profit?
A for-profit business is made to earn money that you can use however you want for your bills, your life, your growth, your healing. You can sell:
- Products (like haircare, food, crafts)
- Services (like cleaning, speaking, teaching, coaching)

You can still help people in a for-profit business. In fact, many heart-led survivors start for-profit businesses that change lives and get paid well for it. That is okay. That is allowed.
- You own the business
- You keep the profits
- You have freedom to grow how you choose

What Is a Nonprofit?

A nonprofit is focused on a mission to serve a group of people or solve a social issue. You don't "own" the nonprofit. It belongs to the community it serves. You might:

1. Offer free support groups
2. Provide education or training
3. Advocate for change or raise awareness

You can still earn a salary as the founder, but the money that comes in must go back into the mission.

- You get to serve a cause
- You can apply for grants and donations
- You may need a board of directors and reports

How Do You Know Which One to Choose?

Ask yourself a few simple questions:
- Do I want full control of how I run my business?
  If yes → For-profit might be better
- Do I want to sell things or get paid for services?
  If yes → For-profit is the path
- Do I want to offer free help to people who can't pay?
  If yes → A nonprofit could be a great fit
- Do I want to apply for grants or donations?
  If yes → You may want a nonprofit

Do I want to do both - make money AND serve people deeply? That's possible too! Some people start with a for-profit and later add a nonprofit (or vice versa). I actually started from a for profit, and six years after, I founded a nonprofit, The Enitan Story. The organization provides direct services to individuals who have experienced human trafficking and domestic violence. It also builds capacity for survivors to become Subject Matter Experts (SMEs) with lived experience.

Real-Life Example
Let's say you want to help teen survivors. You could:
- Start a nonprofit that offers free workshops in schools, or
- Create a for-profit coaching program for teens who want deeper one-on-one support, or
- Do both over time!

What matters most is that you start with what feels doable and meaningful to you right now.

Action Steps: Profit Path Finder
Let's figure out what fits you today.
- What do I want my business to do?
  (Help people? Sell things? Educate? Raise awareness?)
- Do I want to earn a living through this business?
  (Yes? Then for-profit might be your main path.)
- Would I like to serve people who can't pay?
  (If yes, you might explore a nonprofit or donation-based option.)
- What feels lighter to start with?
  (Go with that. You can evolve later!)

Don't worry about getting it perfect. Just get it going. The most important thing is to choose a path that gives you:
- Freedom to grow
- Room to breathe
- A way to serve without burning out

Whether you are for-profit or nonprofit, you are still doing something powerful.

Money is not dirty. Money is not evil. Money is just a tool, and you deserve to use that tool to care for yourself, your family, and your future.

Chapter 5

How to Make It Legal (Without Stress)

Okay visionary, you've got your idea. You know whether you want to start a for-profit or nonprofit. Now comes the part that makes a lot of people freeze: Making it legal. But here's the good news. It's not as scary as it sounds. You don't need a lawyer. You don't need a fancy office. You just need a few basic steps, and I will walk you through them like we are sitting at the kitchen table.
Let's take the mystery and fear out of the process so you can move forward with confidence.

What Does "Making It Legal" Even Mean?
When we say, "make it legal," we mean:
- Giving your business a real name.
- Registering it with the government.
- Getting a number called an EIN (like a Social Security number for your business).
- Opening a bank account just for your business.
- Getting any licenses or permits you need, if necessary for your business type.

You don't have to do it all at once. You can take it step by step. That's the healing way and the visionary way.

Step-by-Step: Starting a For-Profit Business

Here is what you need to do if you are starting a regular business:

- Pick a Name
  Choose something meaningful to you and easy to remember.
- Register Your Business Name
  Go to your state's Secretary of State website (or ask your local small business office) to register the name. This is often called a "DBA" (Doing Business As).
- Choose Your Business Type
  Most people start with:
  ➤ Sole Proprietorship if you're just one person getting started.
  ➤ LLC (Limited Liability Company) if you want legal protection between your business and personal money.
- Get an Employment Identification Number (EIN)
  This is free and easy. Go to the IRS website and apply for an EIN. It's like a Social Security number for your business.
- Open a Business Bank Account
  This keeps your personal and business money separate and it is super important!
- Check for Licenses or Permits
  Some businesses (like food, cleaning, or childcare) may need a local or state license. Ask your city clerk's office or search online.

Step-by-Step: Starting a Nonprofit

If you want to start a nonprofit, here is a simple version of the process:

- **Pick a Name**
  Make sure no one else in your state has the same one.
- **Recruit a Board of Directors**
  Usually, 3 people are required to serve on the board. These people help guide the mission.
- **Write Bylaws**
  This is a simple document that says how your nonprofit will run.
- **File for Nonprofit Status with Your State**
  This gives you official recognition as a nonprofit.
- **Apply for 501(c)(3) Status with the IRS**
  This makes your nonprofit tax-exempt and allows people to give you donations that they can write off. You will also be able to apply for private and public grants to implement the organization's programs.
- **Open a Nonprofit Bank Account**
  This is where your grant money or donations will go.

Yes, it is more steps than a regular business but take it slow. Ask for help. Call your local SCORE, Small Business Development Center (SBDC), or Women's Business Center. They give free help for starting businesses and nonprofits. You can also take classes. I took a class on how to start a successful nonprofit with the Minnesota Council of Nonprofits when I was starting The Enitan Story (TES).

Real Talk: You Don't Have to Do It Alone.
When I started, I had to figure things out step by step. Sometimes I asked for help. Sometimes I made mistakes. But I kept going.

You are allowed to:
- Ask questions
- Watch YouTube tutorials
- Go slow
- Pause when overwhelmed
- Come back and keep going

This is your business, your pace, your power.

Action Steps: Legal Checklist
Here's your simple next step, depending on the kind of business you're starting.

For-Profit Starter List:
- Pick a name
- Register with your state
- Get an EIN from the IRS
- Open a business bank account
- Check if you need a license

Nonprofit Starter List:
- Choose a name
- Form your board
- Write simple bylaws
- Register with your state
- Apply for 501(c)(3) status
- Open a nonprofit bank account

Do one thing this week. Just one. That is all you need to do right now. Making it legal doesn't have to be scary. It just means you're taking yourself and your dream seriously. You are becoming a business owner. You are becoming a leader. And you are doing it your way.

Chapter 6

Set Your Prices with Confidence

Let me tell you something important: It is okay to charge for your work. Let me say that again, slowly: It is okay to be paid. You have been through a lot. You have given so much. And for many survivors, asking for money can feel uncomfortable. Maybe you have been taught to shrink yourself. Maybe you feel guilty. Or maybe you are afraid people won't pay you. But here is what I want you to know: You deserve to be paid for your time, your skill, and your story. You are not greedy. You are not selfish. You are building a life, and that takes resources. Let us walk through how to set your prices with confidence and without fear.

Why Pricing Feels So Hard (Especially for Survivors)
If you have experienced trauma, especially exploitation or abuse, you may have been taught that your value comes from pleasing others, not from knowing your worth. But your business is not about pleasing people. It is about providing value, and value has a price.

Money is not dirty. Money is not evil. Money is just a tool, and you deserve to use that tool to care for yourself, your family, and your future.

How to Set a Simple Starting Price
You don't need to be a math expert. Just start with these 3 things:
1. What does it cost you?
   - Think about your supplies, tools, website, gas, time.
   - Add it all up. That's your cost.
2. What do you want to earn per hour?
   - Think about how much time it takes to make, create, or offer your service.
   - You deserve to pay yourself like any job.
3. What would feel fair for both you and the customer?
   - Check what others charge for similar things (look online).
   - Don't copy, just get an idea of the range.

Then, pick a price that covers your cost, pays you, and feels good in your gut.

Simple Pricing Example
Let's say you make self-care boxes:
- Supplies (tea, candle, card): $10
- Time to pack and ship: 30 minutes
- You want to earn $20/hour → that's $10 for your time
- Total cost: $20

So, your price could be $30, giving you room to cover costs, pay yourself, and save or reinvest.
You are allowed to profit. That is how your business grows.

What If Someone Says "That's Too Expensive"?
Let them. Not everyone is your customer. And that is okay. Some people won't understand your value. That doesn't mean your price is wrong. It just means they are not your people yet. You don't have to chase customers. You just need to stay consistent and speak to the people who understand your heart and your work.

Real Talk: Giving and Charging Can Work Together
It is okay to help people and get paid. You can:
- Offer sliding scale pricing
- Give discounts to survivors
- Do giveaways or free events sometimes

But don't build your whole business on giving everything away. You matter too.

Action Steps: Simple Pricing Starter
Take a few minutes and fill this out:
1. What are you selling or offering?
   (Example: natural body butter)
2. What does it cost to make or deliver?
   (Example: $5 for ingredients, $2 for container = $7 total)
3. How much time does it take?
   (Example: 30 minutes)
4. What do you want to pay yourself for that time?
   (Example: $10)
5. Add it up and set a starting price
   (Example: $7 + $10 = $17 → so charge $20)

Then say it out loud to yourself: "I charge $20 for my product/service, and I am worth it." Say it again. Let it sink in. Let your nervous system learn that it is safe to receive.

Charging money is not selfish, it is sustainable. You're not just building a business. You're building a better future. And you deserve to be paid for it.

Chapter 7

How to Get Your First Customer

Alright, visionary. You've got your idea. You've made it legal. You've even set your prices. Now comes the part that makes it real: Getting your first customer. Let's take a deep breath together. This doesn't have to be scary. You don't need a big website, tons of followers, or business cards (unless you want them). All you need is a clear offer and a willing heart to share it. You already have everything you need to get started right now, today.

Why the First Customer Matters
Your first customer is more than a sale; it is proof that your idea works. It builds your confidence. It gives you momentum. And it helps you get clear on what people really want from you. Even if they are a friend or someone from your community, they still count. Every great business started with one person saying yes. So don't wait until it is perfect. Just get it out there. Let people know how they can support you.

Simple Ways to Get Your First Customer

Here are 5 survivor-friendly ways to find that first paying customer:

Tell Your Story Online: Post on social media (Facebook, Instagram, even WhatsApp!) and say something simple like: "I'm starting my own business helping people feel confident with natural skincare. I just launched my first product, and I'd love your support! Here's what I'm offering…" Include a photo, a short description, and your price.

Ask Your Circle: Reach out to 5 people you trust. Say something like: "Hey, I just launched my business. I thought of you because you've always supported me. Would you be interested or know someone who might be?" Sometimes your first sale comes from someone who already believes in you.

Share in Community Groups: Join local Facebook groups, survivor networks, or church groups and share your offer (if allowed). Focus on helping, not just selling.

Offer a Sample or Trial: If you feel nervous about charging full price, offer a small version of your product or a short version of your service. Let them try it and ask for feedback or a testimonial!

Be Visible: You don't have to shout. Just be seen:
- Wear a shirt with your brand name
- Carry your product when you go out
- Talk about your business casually when people ask what you do

You never know who is watching, or who is waiting for what you offer.

Real Example: From Vision to Sale

When I first started Bukola Braiding & Beauty Supply, I approached women individually, telling them that I could braid hair. One by one with word of mouth, customers began to show up to have their hair braided. And little by little, it grew. That is how it starts. With one brave share. One tiny yes.

Simple Script You Can Use

You can copy this or tweak it for your own voice: "Hi, my name is [Your Name]. I'm a survivor and visionary starting a new business to [what you do]. I just launched my first [product/service] and I'd love to invite you to check it out. If you or someone you know could use [what it offers], I'd be so grateful for your support!"

Action Steps: First Customer Plan

Let's map it out. Just one small step at a time.

- **What am I offering right now?**
  (Example: 4oz herbal body butter for $20)
- **Who do I know that might need this, or know someone who does?**
  (Write down 5 names)
- **What platform or place can I share it today?**
  (Example: Facebook, text message, church group, local pop-up)
- **What will I say when I talk about it?**
  (Use the simple script above or write your own)

Now, go and share it with just one person. That is all. And remember, you are not being pushy. You are offering a solution. You are showing up for your dream.

Your first customer is the first brick in your foundation. Start small. Stay honest. Keep going. You don't need a crowd. You just need a start. And that start is waiting for you today.

Chapter 8

Make Your Brand Shine So People Can Find You

Now that you've got your first offer (or maybe even your first sale), it's time to think about branding and visibility. This is just a fancy way of asking: "How will people know I exist and what I offer?" Don't worry, this isn't about being loud or flashy. This is about being clear, authentic, and visible in a way that feels good to you. Your brand is your voice, your vibe, your values. And your visibility is how you show up so people can find you and support you. Let's break it down, survivor-strength style.

What Is Branding?
Branding is how people experience your business. It's:
- What you say
- How you look
- What you stand for

Think of it like the "personality" of your business. If you had a business called "Ewa Natural Skincare," your brand might be:
- Calm, gentle, healing
- Focused on beauty from the inside out
- Bright colors, plant-based ingredients, African roots

Your brand should feel like YOU. You don't have to copy anyone else. You don't need to be perfect. You just need to be real.

What Is Visibility?
Visibility means people can:
- Find you
- Understand what you do
- Trust you

You don't need a fancy website to be visible. You just need a way to show up consistently in front of the right people.

3 Simple Ways to Build Your Brand
Pick 1–2 Colors and Fonts
Keep it simple. Choose colors you love and a clean, easy-to-read font. You can use tools like Canva to create simple flyers or social media posts with your brand look.

Use a Consistent Profile Picture or Logo
Whether it's your face or a logo, use the same image everywhere on social media, WhatsApp, flyers, etc. It helps people recognize you.

Have a Short Tagline
A short sentence that explains what you do. For example:
"Healing through handmade skincare."
"Affordable wellness for survivors."
"Haircare made with love and herbs."
This helps people instantly know what you're about.

3 Simple Ways to Be Visible

Show Up Online (Even If You're Shy)
Post once or twice a week on social media or send a message to your community. Share:
- A behind-the-scenes photo
- A tip or quote
- Your product or service

Just be real. That's what people connect with.

Share Flyers in Your Community
Print a simple flyer with your name, what you offer, your phone number or social handle, and a photo. Ask to leave it at:
- Salons
- Churches
- Local stores
- Clinics or community centers

Talk About It Naturally
When someone asks, "What do you do?" say: "I run a small business that helps people with…" Or "I create handmade products for…"

Practice until it feels natural. You are not selling, you are sharing.

Real Talk: You Don't Have to Be Everywhere
You don't need TikTok, YouTube, Instagram, and a website all at once. Pick one or two platforms or spaces where your people are and be consistent. It is better to show up regularly in one place than to burn out trying to be everywhere.

Action Steps: Brand & Visibility Builder

- **What do I want people to feel when they see my brand?**
  (Example: Calm, bold, joyful, safe...)
- **What colors or images represent that feeling?**
  (Example: Green for healing, gold for royalty, a leaf symbol...)
- **What do I want people to say when they describe my business?**
  (Example: "She makes the best natural products," "She really helps people feel seen...")

  Where will I show up this week so people can find me?
  (Example: Facebook post, flyer at local salon, word of mouth...)

Your brand is your light. Your visibility is your voice. You don't need to be loud. You just need to be clear, true, and present. People are looking for what you carry. Let them see you.

Chapter 9

How to Talk About Your Business (Without Feeling Salesy)

Let's be honest: Talking about your business can feel awkward. Especially if you've spent years being told to stay quiet… Or if you were taught that asking for support is "too much"… Or if you feel like you're not "good at selling." Here's the truth, dear visionary: You don't have to be a salesperson. You just have to be you. People don't buy from perfect people. They buy from people they trust. They buy from people who are real.

Let's walk through how to talk about your business with confidence and clarity without ever feeling fake.

What Makes Something Feel "Salesy"?
- Talking too much about yourself
- Pushing someone to buy when they're not ready
- Sounding like a robot or a commercial

That's not your style. And guess what? It doesn't have to be.

What Makes Something Feel Genuine?
- Sharing your story
- Offering something helpful
- Being honest and clear
- Inviting people, not pressuring them

People want to connect and not be sold to.

Simple Ways to Talk About Your Business (That Feel Natural)

Use "Helping" Language
Instead of: "I sell skincare products."
Try: "I help people feel confident in their skin using natural products."

Instead of: "I charge $50 for coaching."
Try: "I work with people who are rebuilding their lives. My coaching supports healing, confidence, and starting over."

You are not just selling, you are serving.

Share Why You Started
Your story is your strength. Try this: "As a survivor, I know how hard it is to find peace and confidence. That was why I started my business, to give others what I wish I had."
People will remember that more than any sales pitch.

Use the "Feel, Do, Get" Formula
This helps you clearly explain what you do in a way people understand.
I help [who] feel [emotion] so they can [result].

Example: "I help survivors feel supported so they can heal and move forward with confidence." This makes it about them and not just your product.

Practice Short Scripts for Different Moments

At a networking event or party: "I run a small business creating herbal skincare. It's all about healing from the outside in."

On social media: "Starting my business helped me find my voice. Now I help others do the same through coaching and support."

When someone asks, "What do you do?" You respond with, "I use my lived experience to help others heal and grow. My business is part of that journey." You don't need to be perfect. You just need to be real.

Roleplay Time: You Got This

Imagine someone just said: "Tell me about your business!" Take a deep breath and try saying: "Thanks for asking! I help [who] with [what you do], using [what makes you unique]. I started because [short story]. Right now, I'm offering [product/service]. Would you like to learn more?"

Simple. Heartfelt. No pressure.

Action Steps: Confidence Script Builder

Take a moment to answer these questions:
- **Who do I help?**
  (Example: Women who've been through trauma)
- **What do I offer them?**
  (Example: Handmade self-care products, emotional support, or education)

- Why did I start?
  (Example: I wanted to turn my pain into purpose)
- **How do people benefit from working with me?**
  (Example: They feel seen, supported, and empowered

Now, put it all together in one sentence that you can practice:
"I help _____ by _____ so they can _____. I started because _____."
Practice saying it out loud until it feels natural. Try it in front of the mirror. Say it to a friend. Say it to your phone. The more you say it, the more confident you'll feel.

You are not bothering people, you are blessing them with your gifts. You're not selling. You're sharing your heart. And when your heart is in it, people will feel it.

Chapter 10

Build a Business That Supports Your Healing

When I started my business, I thought I had to be "strong" all the time. I thought I had to push through, hustle, and hide my pain. But over time, I learned this: A business that doesn't care for your healing will burn you out. A business that honors your healing will build your future. You did not survive all you have been through just to recreate stress and exhaustion.

You are allowed to build a business that supports your:
- Healing
- Rest
- Boundaries
- Joy
- Growth

Let's talk about how to do that step by step.

Healing Comes First
You are a whole person and not just a business owner.

You bring your story, your energy, and your heart into everything you do. That means you have to protect your peace, not just your profits. Give yourself the permission to:
- Take breaks
- Say no to things that don't feel good
- ·Pause when your body says pause
- Ask for help
- Rest without guilt

You don't need to "earn" your healing. It's your birthright.

Build Slowly and Safely
Your business doesn't have to grow fast to be successful. Go slow. Go steady. Go safely. I am still at it for close to two decades and I am still going within my pace, rather than trying to be someone else. Slow and steady, builds authenticity and longevity faster. Start with:
- A simple offer
- A few trusted clients
- One or two platforms

As your healing grows, your business will grow with it. And when you need to pull back? That is okay too.

Set Healthy Boundaries
Boundaries are like walls around your garden. They protect the good things growing inside. Try setting clear limits around:
- Your time (set work hours, even if you work from home)
- Your emotional energy (not every client deserves your whole story)
- Your space (have a spot just for work if you can)

You get to say:
"I'm not available right now."
"That doesn't work for me."
"I need time to think about that."
"I don't share that part of my story publicly."
Boundaries are not rude, they are responsible.

Make Room for Joy and Support

Your business should include moments of joy. Even if it is just lighting a candle before you work, listening to music while you create, or celebrating every little win. Also, don't do it alone. Find support:
- A therapist
- A mentor or coach
- A survivor business circle
- A friend who believes in you

You are not weak for needing support. You're wise.

Action Steps: Healing-Centered Business Check-In

Answer these questions with honesty and care:

How does my business feel in my body right now, heavy or light?
(If it feels heavy, what needs to shift?)

Am I getting enough rest and care while building my business?
(What can I do to make more space for healing?)

Where do I need to set a boundary - time, energy, money, emotions?
(Write one sentence you can use to hold that boundary.)

What brings me joy in my business?
(How can I do more of that?)

Who can I ask for support this week?
(Reach out, even if it is just to say, "I'm trying.")

Your business should heal you, not hurt you.
You don't have to push.
You don't have to hide.

You get to build something that honors all of who you are.
From trauma to triumph.
From pain to purpose.
From victim to visionary.

Final Words: Your Business Is Just the Beginning
You did not read this book by accident. You are not dreaming this dream by mistake. You are ready. Not perfect. Not polished. But ready. And that's enough. So, take the next step. Launch that idea. Share your story. Make your product. Serve your people. And if you fall or fumble along the way? That is part of the journey too. You are not just building a business. You are building your life, one choice, one chapter, one dream at a time. I see you. I believe in you. And I'll be cheering you on the whole way.

Bonus Resource
Use the worksheets at the end of each chapter to build your very own Survivor Business Plan. You can go back anytime and fill in the blanks, take notes, or share it with a mentor or coach. You can download the pdf format of the worksheet at https://bukolaoriola.com/bukolaoriolagroup/.

This is your story. This is your start. And the world is waiting for what you carry.

Bukola Oriola's Work

BUKOLA ORIOLA GROUP (BOG), LLC

Bukola Oriola Group, LLC offers expert consultation to individuals, nonprofit and for-profit organizations, and government agencies on combating human trafficking and domestic violence, providing personalized solutions, training, policy guidance, and strategic planning.

The media arm focuses on both print and video content. We produce books, reports, and educational materials on human trafficking, domestic violence, social justice, and entrepreneurship to raise awareness, educate the public, and support individuals with lived experience, organizations, and policymakers.

Additionally, BOG creates and distribute engaging videos on social issues such as human trafficking, domestic violence, survivor stories, advocacy, and social entrepreneurship through platforms like YouTube, social media, and our website.
Furthermore, the company produces video content that discusses and raises awareness about human trafficking, domestic violence, and social entrepreneurship, featuring interviews with Subject Matter Experts (SME) with lived experience, other professionals in the field, and activists, as well as investigative reports and educational segments.

Bukola Oriola's Work

THE ENITAN STORY

The Enitan Story (TES) operates from a survivor informed and subject matter expert with lived experience point of view.
The organization provides unique and individualized services to individuals who have experienced or at risk for domestic violence and human trafficking/exploitation (labor and sex) across various ages, race, and gender across the state of Minnesota and beyond.

The organization's program focuses on:
- Outreach & Advocacy
- Case Management
- Training for nonprofit& for Profit organizations
- Job & Life Skills for traditional job or entrepreneurship
- Referrals for comprehensive services
- Capacity building for survivors to become subject matter experts with lived experience.

Work with Bukola Oriola

You can request to work with Bukola Oriola. She is available to help you start or leverage your business through:
- One-on-one, or group coaching.
- Book Publishing.
- Training, and more.

> *Boundaries are like walls around your garden. They protect the good things growing inside. You get to say:*
> *"I'm not available right now."*
> *"That doesn't work for me."*
> *"I need time to think about that."*
> *"I don't share that part of my story publicly."*
> *Boundaries are not rude, they are responsible.*

OTHER TITLES BY BUKOLA ORIOLA

- Imprisoned: The Travails of a Trafficked Victim.
- A Living Label: An Inspirational Memoir and Guide.
- Quit Your Day Job!: Five steps to turn your passion to money using blogging and social media.
- I Declare: Beauty and Wellness Morning Affirmations.
- Make Your Book A Best Seller: The Step-by-Step Guide I followed to Become a #1 Amazon Bestseller in Multiple Countries.
- The Natural Hair Softness Headaches: 6 items in your kitchen or drug store you will find helpful.
- Bringing the Story Back Home: Implementing Change with Human Trafficking Awareness.
- Simple Steps to Hair Braiding
- L Magazine (Lipstick, Lip Balm & Literacy).
- I Declare Gratitude
- I Declare Hope

www.ingramcontent.com/pod-product-compliance
Lightning Source LLC
Chambersburg PA
CBHW070950180426
43194CB00041B/2039